THE HOUSE OF BERNARDA ALBA

A Drama About Women
in Villages of Spain

BY FEDERICO
GARCÍA LORCA

ADAPTED IN ENGLISH BY
EMILY MANN

★

★
DRAMATISTS
PLAY SERVICE
INC.

THE HOUSE OF BERNARDA ALBA
(La Casa de Bernarda Alba)
Translation by Emily Mann Copyright ©
Emily Mann and Herederos de Federico García Lorca
based on *La Casa de Bernarda Alba* by Federico García Lorca
Copyright © Herederos de Federico García Lorca

All Rights Reserved

SPECIAL NOTE

THE HOUSE OF BERNARDA ALBA
(La Casa de Bernarda Alba)

by Federico García Lorca
in a new version by Emily Mann

CHARACTERS

BERNARDA — (age 60)
MARIA JOSEFA — Bernarda's mother (age 80)
ANGUSTIAS — Bernarda's daughter (age 39)
MAGDALENA — Bernarda's daughter (age 30)
AMELIA — Bernarda's daughter (age 27)
MARTIRIO — Bernarda's daughter (age 24)
ADELA — Bernarda's daughter (age 20)
A MAID — (age 50)
LA PONCIA — a maid (age 60)
PRUDENCIA — (age 50)
A BEGGAR WOMAN and LITTLE GIRL
WOMEN IN MOURNING

In Ms. Mann's production, the entire play takes place in the court-yard of Bernarda Alba's house. There is no intermission.

The writer states that the play is intended as a photographic document.

PLEASE NOTE — Most of the stage directions appear as they do in Lorca's original text; *however,* stage directions printed as footnotes reflect staging choices made by Emily Mann for her production at McCarter Theatre.

THE HOUSE OF BERNARDA ALBA
A Drama About Women
in the Villages of Spain

ACT ONE

It is summer. A great brooding silence fills the stage. It is empty when the curtain rises. Bells can be heard tolling outside.

MAID. *(Entering.)* The sound of those bells hits me right between the eyes.

PONCIA. *(She enters, eating bread and sausage.)* They've been mumbling away for over two hours. The church looks beautiful ... When they sang the first response for the dead, Magdalena fainted.

MAID. She's the one left most alone.

PONCIA. She's the only one her father loved. *(She eats.)*

MAID. If Bernarda sees you ...

PONCIA. Since she's not eating today, she'd like us all to die of starvation. The old tyrant! Well, I'll fool her. I came back to open a jar of sausages.

MAID. Poncia, can I have some for my little girl?

PONCIA. Help yourself and take a fistful of beans while you're at it. She won't notice the difference today.

MARIA JOSEFA. *(Voice off.)* Bernarda!

PONCIA. Is the old lady locked in?

MAID. Double locked. I put the bar down. She can pick a lock.

MARIA JOSEFA. *(Voice off.)* Bernarda!

PONCIA. *(Yelling.)* She's coming! *(To the Maid.)* Make sure everything's spotless. If Bernarda doesn't see it shine, she'll pull out the few hairs I've got left in my head.

MAID. That woman!

PONCIA. Tyrant over everyone around her. She is capable of sitting on your heart and watching you die for a whole year without taking that cold smile off her wicked face. "Scrub, scrub those floors!"

MAID. My hands are bloody from all the scrubbing.

PONCIA. Oh she's the cleanest, the most decent, she's superior to us all. Her poor husband earned a good rest. *(The bells stop.)*

MAID. Are there enough chairs?

PONCIA. Plenty. Let them sit on the floor. She doesn't like people under her roof anyway. Nobody's been to this house since her father died. She's mean.

MAID. With you, she behaves well.

PONCIA. Thirty years washing her sheets; thirty years eating her leftovers; nights watching over her when she had a cough; whole days peeking through a crack in the shutters to spy on the neighbors and tell her the tale; life without secrets one from the other. Curse her. May the nails of the cross pierce both her eyes.

MAID. Poncia!

PONCIA. But I'm a good dog. I bark when I'm told to, and I bite the beggars' heels when she sics me on them. My boys may work in her fields — but the day will come when I've had enough.

MAID. And then...?

PONCIA. And then I'll lock myself in a room with her and spit in her face — for a whole year. "Here's for this, Bernarda, and here's for that, and here's for the other" till I leave her like a lizard the boys have squashed. Because that's what she is — her and her whole family. Not that I envy her her life. Stuck with five girls, five ugly daughters — all of them poor — except the eldest, Angustias, by the first husband, she's got some money; but the rest ... oh plenty of embroidered lace and linen tablecloths, but bread and grapes is all they'll inherit.

MAID. I'd like to have what they've got!

PONCIA. *(At the table.)* This glass has some spots on it.

MAID. Nothing will clean it off. *(The bells toll.)*

PONCIA. The last prayer for the dead, I'm going over to listen. There is nobody like the old Sacristan, Tronchafinos. At my mother's mass, God rest her soul, the walls shook, and when he sang the Amen, it was like a wolf had come into the church. *(Imitates.)* A-a-a-a-me-e-en!! *(She starts coughing.)*

MAID. Watch out, you'll pulverize your throat.

PONCIA. I'd rather pulverize something else. *(Goes out laughing. The Maid scrubs. The bells toll.)*

MAID. *(Imitating the bells.)* Dong, dong, dong. May God forgive you! Dong, dong, dong. May you wait many years for me. *(At the door with a Little Girl, a Beggar Woman with her hand out murmurs "Blessed be God" ...)*

The door to the street's right behind you. Any scraps today are mine. *(Beggar Woman enters, shoves the child in to beg on her knees.)*

Get out! Out! Who said you could come in here? Tracking your filthy feet over my clean floor! Get out! Get out! Out! Out! Out! Get out! *(The Beggar Woman and the Little Girl leave. The Maid goes on scrubbing.)*

Linen tablecloths and cupboards while we eat off dirt floors with one plate and one spoon. I pray for the day when not one of us is left to speak of it. *(Bells.)*

Yes, ring away! Let them lift you in a silk-lined coffin with gold handles — you're no less dead than I will be. To hell with you, Antonio Maria Benavides, lying there stiff in your wool suit and your tall boots: Take what's coming to you! You won't be lifting my skirts anymore behind the barn door! *(Laughs. Doors open. Two by two, 200 women* in mourning with large shawls and black skirts and fans begin to enter.)*

Ay! Antonio Maria Benavides, you will never see these walls, you will never break bread under this roof again! I was the one who loved you most of all who served you! *(Pulling her hair.)*

Must I go on living after you're gone? Must I go on living? *(200 women stop. Enter Bernarda and her five daughters. Bernarda leans on her cane.)*

---

* In Mann's production there were twenty women.

BERNARDA. *(Screams to the Maid.)* Silence!

MAID. *(Crying.)* Bernarda!

BERNARDA. Less wailing and more work. You should have had all this clean by now. Get out. You don't belong here. *(The Maid exits, crying.)* The poor are like animals: They're made of different stuff.

PRUDENCIA. *(Indirectly.)* The poor feel their sorrows too.

BERNARDA. But they forget them soon enough over a plate of beans. *(To all.)* Sit down. *(Magdalena cries.)* Magdalena, don't cry. If you want to cry, go do it under your bed. Did you hear me? *(Long pause.)*

PRUDENCIA. I haven't felt heat like this in years. *(Long pause. They all fan themselves.)*

BERNARDA. Is the lemonade ready?

PONCIA. Yes, Bernarda. *(She gets a tray of little white jars.)*

BERNARDA. Give the men some.

PONCIA. They're already drinking, in the yard.

BERNARDA. Let them out the way they came. I don't want them tracking through here. *(Awkward pause.)*

PRUDENCIA. *(To Angustias.)* Pepe el Romano was with the men during the mass, Angustias.

ANGUSTIAS. Yes, he was there.

BERNARDA. His mother was there. She saw his mother. Neither she nor I saw Pepe. *(Women buzz.)* Women in church must not look at a man, unless it is the priest, and only then because he's wearing a skirt. If you turn your head, it means you're itching for the touch of corduroy. *(Women buzz again.)*

PONCIA. *(Between her teeth to the women.)* Twisted old vine ... itching for the heat of a man!

BERNARDA. *(Beats with her cane on the floor once.)* Blessed be God!

ALL. *(Crossing themselves.)* Bless Him and praise Him forever!

BERNARDA. Rest in peace, with the souls of the departed watching over you ...

ALL. Rest in peace!

BERNARDA. With the Archangel Michael and his sword of justice ...

ALL. Rest in peace!

BERNARDA. With the key that opens and the hand that locks ...

ALL. Rest in peace!

BERNARDA. With the most blessed saints, and the little lights of the field ...

ALL. Rest in peace!

BERNARDA. With our holy charity, and with all souls on land and on sea ...

ALL. Rest in peace!

BERNARDA. Grant rest to your servant Antonio Maria Benavides, and crown him with your sacred glory.

ALL. Amen.

BERNARDA. *(She rises and chants.) Requiem aeternam dona eis, Domine.*

ALL. *(Standing and chanting in the Gregorian fashion.) Et lux perpetua luceat eis. (They cross themselves. They start filing out.)*

PONCIA. *(She enters, carrying a moneybag.)* From the men — money for the mass.

BERNARDA. Thank them, give them some brandy. *(A Young Woman hugs Magdalena. To Magdalena, who is starting to cry.)* Ssh! *(She beats with her cane on the floor. All the women have gone out. To the women who have just left.)* Go on back to your caves and criticize everything you've seen! And I hope it'll be many years before you pass through my door again!

PONCIA. You've got nothing to complain about. The whole village came.

BERNARDA. Yes, to fill my house with the sweat from their underclothes and the poison of their tongues.

AMELIA. Mother, don't talk like that!

BERNARDA. What other way can I talk about this damned village, a village without a river, a village full of wells, so every time you drink the water you're afraid it's been poisoned.

PONCIA. Look what they did to the floor! *(Poncia cleans the floor.)*

BERNARDA. Like a herd of goats had tracked through here. Give me a fan, child. *(She gives her a round fan with green and red flowers.)*

ADELA. Take this one.

9

BERNARDA.   Is that the fan you give a widow? *(Throwing the fan on the floor.)* Give me a black one and learn to respect your father's memory.

MARTIRIO.   Take mine.

BERNARDA.   What about you?

MARTIRIO.   I'm not hot.

BERNARDA.   Well, look for another one, you'll need it. For the eight years we'll be in mourning, not even the wind from the street will enter this house. That's how it was in my father's house and in my grandfather's house. Pretend we bricked up all the doors and windows. In the meantime, you will start sewing your trousseaus. There are twenty bolts of linen in the chest from which to cut sheets and coverlets. Magdalena can embroider them.

MAGDALENA.   It makes no difference to me.

ADELA.   *(Sour.)* If you don't want to embroider ours, yours will look better.

MAGDALENA.   Neither mine nor yours. I know I'm never going to get married. I'd rather carry sacks to the mill. Anything rather than sit in these dark rooms day after day.

BERNARDA.   That's what a woman does.

MAGDALENA.   Damn women!

BERNARDA.   In this house you will do as I tell you. You can't run telling tales to your father now. Needle and thread for the woman, whip and mule for the man. That's how it is for people born to certain obligations. *(Adela goes out.)*

MARIA JOSEFA.   *(Voice off.)* Bernarda! Let me out!

BERNARDA.   *(Calling.)* Let her out now! *(The Maid enters.)*

MAID.   I could barely hold her down. She may be eighty years old, but your mother's as strong as an oak tree.

BERNARDA.   It runs in the family. My grandmother was the same.

MAID.   Several times during the wake, I had to put a sack in her mouth. She wanted to shout out to you to let her have some dishwater to drink and some dog meat. That's what she says you feed her.

MARTIRIO.   She's wicked.

BERNARDA.   *(To Maid.)* Let her get some fresh air in the yard.

MAID.   She took all her rings out of her trunk and her amethyst earrings, put them on, and told me she wants to get married. *(The daughters laugh.)*

BERNARDA.   Stay with her. Be careful she doesn't go near the well.

MAID.   You don't have to worry she'll throw herself in.

BERNARDA.   I don't ... that's where the neighbors can see from their window. *(The Maid leaves.)*

MARTIRIO.   We're going to change our clothes.

BERNARDA.   *(Pause.)* All right. *(Adela enters.)* And Angustias?

ADELA.   *(Meaningfully.)* I saw her peering through the crack in the back door. The men have just left.

BERNARDA.   What were you doing at the back door?

ADELA.   I went to see if the hens had laid.

BERNARDA.   But the men had already left?

ADELA.   *(Meaningfully.)* A group of them were still standing around outside.

BERNARDA.   *(Furiously.)* Angustias! Angustias!

ANGUSTIAS.   *(Entering.)* Do you want something?

BERNARDA.   What, or rather at whom, were you looking?

ANGUSTIAS.   Nobody.

BERNARDA.   Do you think it's decent for a woman of your class to throw herself at a man the day of her father's funeral? Answer me! Who were you looking at? *(Pause.)*

ANGUSTIAS.   I ...

BERNARDA.   You!

ANGUSTIAS.   Nobody.

BERNARDA.   *(Goes forward with her cane.)* You spineless...! Sickening slut! *(She strikes her.)*

PONCIA.   *(Running towards her.)* Bernarda! *(She holds her. Angustias cries.)*

BERNARDA.   Get out, all of you! *(They all go out.)*

PONCIA.   She didn't realize what she was doing. Of course, I was shocked to see her sneaking off to the back door, and later she stood at the window, listening to the men's conversation. As usual, it wasn't the kind of conversation one should listen to.

BERNARDA.   That is why they come to funerals. *(With curiosity.)* What were they talking about?

PONCIA.   About Paca la Roseta. Last night they tied her husband up in a stall, threw her over the back of a horse and carried her off to the highest part of the olive grove.

BERNARDA.   So what did she do?

PONCIA.   She? She was willing. They say she was showing her breasts, and Maximiliano played her like a guitar. It was terrible.

BERNARDA.   Then what happened?

PONCIA.   What had to happen. They came back almost at dawn. Paca La Roseta had her hair loose, a crown of flowers on her head.

BERNARDA.   She's the only bad woman we have in the village.

PONCIA.   Because she's not from here. And the men who were with her are the sons of outsiders too. The men from here are not capable of that.

BERNARDA.   No, but they like to watch, talk about it, suck their fingers over it.

PONCIA.   They were saying other things, too.

BERNARDA.   *(Looking from side to side.)* Such as?

PONCIA.   I'm embarrassed to say.

BERNARDA.   And Angustias heard them?

PONCIA.   Of course.

BERNARDA.   That one takes after her aunts, all innocent and flirtatious, making big sheep's eyes at the first nobody who pays her a compliment. Oh, what you have to put up with, the fight you have to wage to make them behave decently and not run wild.

PONCIA.   It's just that your girls are at an age when they should have husbands. They don't give you any trouble. Angustias must be well over thirty by now.

BERNARDA.   She's thirty-nine to be precise.

PONCIA.   Imagine. And she's never had a sweetheart ...

BERNARDA.   *(Furious.)* No, none of them have had a sweetheart, and they don't miss them. They get along very well.

PONCIA.   I didn't mean to offend you.

BERNARDA.   There's no one good enough to come near them for a hundred miles around. The men in this town are not of their class. Do you want me to turn them over to the first farmhand I see?

PONCIA.   You should have moved to another town.

BERNARDA.   Oh, I see. To sell them.

PONCIA.   No, Bernarda. A change ... Of course, in any other place they'd be the poor ones.

BERNARDA.   Stop tormenting me!

PONCIA.   No one can talk to you. Do we or do we not confide in each other?

BERNARDA.   We do not. You serve me, I pay you. Nothing more.

MAID.   *(Entering.)* Don Arturo is here. He's come to see about the will.

BERNARDA.   Let's go. *(To the Maid.)* You start sweeping out the yard. *(To Poncia.)* And you start putting the dead man's clothes away in the big chest.

PONCIA.   We could give some things away.

BERNARDA.   Nothing! Not even a button! Not even the handkerchief we covered his face with! *(She goes out slowly, leaning on her cane. At the door she turns to look at her two servants. They go out. She leaves. Amelia and Martirio enter.)*

AMELIA.   Did you take your medicine?

MARTIRIO.   For all the good it'll do me.

AMELIA.   But you took it.

MARTIRIO.   I do things without believing in them. But like clockwork.

AMELIA.   Since the new doctor came, you're much livelier.

MARTIRIO.   I feel the same.

AMELIA.   Did you notice? Adelaida wasn't at the funeral.

MARTIRIO.   I know. Her fiancé won't let her go out, not even to the front door. She used to be happy; now she doesn't even powder her face.

AMELIA.   These days you don't know if it's better to have a fiancé or not.

MARTIRIO.   It doesn't matter.

AMELIA.   It's the fault of that harpy who won't let us live. Adelaida is going to have a terrible time.

MARTIRIO.   Do you know how afraid she is of Mother?

AMELIA.   What?

MARTIRIO. Because Mother's the only one who knows how her father got his land.

AMELIA. What do you mean?

MARTIRIO. Adelaida's father killed his first wife's husband so he could marry her himself.

AMELIA. *(Whispers.)* My God!

MARTIRIO. Then he left her and went off with another woman who had a daughter, and later he had an affair with the daughter!

AMELIA. Adelaida's mother!

MARTIRIO. And married *her* after the second wife died insane.

AMELIA. Why isn't a man like that put in jail?

MARTIRIO. Because men help each other and cover up for each other so no one is able to tell on them.

AMELIA. But none of this is Adelaida's fault.

MARTIRIO. No, but history repeats itself. It's better never to look at a man. I've been afraid of them since I was a little girl. I used to watch them in the corral, yoking the bullocks, lifting the sacks of grain, with their loud voices and heavy boots ... and always I was afraid of getting older for fear that I would suddenly find myself ... in their arms. God made me weak and ugly and kept them away from me.

AMELIA. You can't say that. Enrique Humanes was after you and you liked him.

MARTIRIO. That's only what people thought! One time I stood in my nightgown at the window until daybreak, because he sent the field hand's little girl to tell me he'd be coming, and he didn't come. It was all talk. Then he married someone else, with more than me.

AMELIA. And ugly as the day is long.

MARTIRIO. What do men care about ugliness? All that matters to them is land, yokes of oxen, and a submissive bitch who'll give them something to eat.

AMELIA. Shh! *(Magdalena enters.)*

MAGDALENA. What are you doing?

MARTIRIO. Sitting here.

AMELIA. What about you?

14

MAGDALENA. I've been going through the rooms for the exercise and to look at the needlepoint pictures Grandmother made; the little woolly dog, and the black man wrestling the lion — we liked them so much when we were children. That was a happier time. A wedding lasted ten days and vicious tongues weren't in style. Today, it's more proper. Brides wear white veils just like in the cities and we drink wine from bottles, but we're rotting away inside these walls because we're afraid of what people might say.

AMELIA. Your shoelace is untied.

MAGDALENA. What of it?

AMELIA. You'll trip on it and fall.

MAGDALENA. Well, that'll be one less.

MARTIRIO. Where's Adela?

MAGDALENA. She put on the green dress she made to wear for her birthday, and went out into the yard, shouting, "Chickens, chickens, look at me!" I had to laugh.

AMELIA. If Mother had seen her!

MAGDALENA. Poor thing! Because she's the youngest, she still has dreams. I'd give anything to see her happy. *(Pause. Angustias crosses the stage, carrying towels.)*

ANGUSTIAS. What time is it?

MAGDALENA. Well it must be twelve.

ANGUSTIAS. That late?

AMELIA. It's about to strike. *(Angustias goes out.)*

MAGDALENA. *(Meaningfully.)* Do you know about it yet? *(Pointing to Angustias, with intent.)*

AMELIA. No.

MAGDALENA. Come on.

MARTIRIO. I don't know what you're talking about ...

MAGDALENA. You both know better than I, always with your heads together like two little sheep, not letting anyone in on things. About Pepe el Romano!

MARTIRIO. Ah!

MAGDALENA. *(Mocking her.)* Ah! The whole village is talking about it. Pepe el Romano is going to marry Angustias. He was lurking around the house last night and I think he's going to send a declaration soon.

15

MARTIRIO.   I'm glad. He's a good man.

AMELIA.   So am I. Angustias has good qualities.

MAGDALENA.   Neither one of you is glad.

MARTIRIO.   Magdalena! Please!

MAGDALENA.   If he were coming because of her looks, for Angustias as a woman, I'd be glad. But he's coming for her money. Even though Angustias is our sister, we're her family and we all know that she's old and sick and has always been the least attractive one of us all. If she looked like a scarecrow when she was twenty; what does she look like now she's nearly forty!

MARTIRIO.   Don't talk like that. Good fortune comes to the one who least expects it.

AMELIA.   But Magdalena's right! Angustias has all her own father's money; she's the only rich one in this house. And that's why, now that our father's dead and all his money's going to be divided, they're coming after her.

MAGDALENA.   Pepe el Romano is twenty-five and the best looking man in this village. The natural thing would be for him to go after you, Amelia, or Adela who's twenty, not the least likely person in the house, a woman who — just like her father — talks through her nose.

MARTIRIO.   Maybe he likes it.

MAGDALENA.   I've never been able to stomach your hypocrisy.

MARTIRIO.   Oh, God! *(Adela enters, in her green dress.)*

MAGDALENA.   Did the chickens see your dress?

ADELA.   What do you want me to do?

AMELIA.   If mother sees you she'll tear your hair out.

ADELA.   I had such hopes for this dress. I was going to wear it when we went to eat melons by the waterwheel. There wouldn't have been another one like it.

MARTIRIO.   It's a lovely dress.

ADELA.   And it looks good on me. It's the best Magdalena's ever cut.

MAGDALENA.   And the chickens? What did they say to you?

ADELA.   They presented me with a few fleas that bit my legs. *(They all laugh.)*

MARTIRIO. You could dye it black.

MAGDALENA. The best thing you can do is give it to Angustias for her wedding to Pepe el Romano.

ADELA. *(With hidden emotion.)* But Pepe el Romano ...

AMELIA. Haven't you heard?

ADELA. No.

MAGDALENA. Well, now you know.

ADELA. But that's not possible ...

MAGDALENA. Money makes anything possible.

ADELA. Is that why she went out after the wake, why she was standing at the door? *(Pause.)* And that man would be capable of ...

MAGDALENA. ... anything. *(Pause.)*

MARTIRIO. What are you thinking, Adela?

ADELA. I'm thinking this period of mourning has caught me at the worst possible moment.

MAGDALENA. You'll get used to it.

ADELA. *(Bursting out, crying with rage.)* No, I will not get used to it. I can't stay locked up. I don't want to shrivel up like you, I don't want to lose the whiteness of my skin in these rooms. Tomorrow I am going to put on my green dress and go walking in the street. I want to go out! *(The Maid enters.)*

MAGDALENA. *(With authority.)* Adela!

MAID. Poor thing, she misses her father. *(The Maid exits.)*

MARTIRIO. Quiet.

AMELIA. What happens to one of us happens to all of us. *(Adela calms herself.)*

MAGDALENA. The maid almost heard you. *(The Maid enters again.)*

MAID. Pepe el Romano is coming down the street. *(Amelia, Martirio and Magdalena run hurriedly.)*

MAGDALENA. Let's go see him! *(They leave rapidly.)*

MAID. *(To Adela.)* Not going?

ADELA. It doesn't make any difference to me.

MAID. He has to come around the corner, you can see best from the window in your room. *(The Servant goes out. Adela is left on the stage, standing doubtfully; after a moment, she also leaves rapidly, going toward her room. Bernarda and La Poncia come in.)*

17

BERNARDA. Curse this ... parceling-out.

PONCIA. There's a lot of money for Angustias.

BERNARDA. Yes.

PONCIA. A whole lot less for the others.

BERNARDA. You've said that to me three times, when you know I do not want it even mentioned. "Much less, a whole lot less." Don't remind me of it ever again. *(Angustias comes in, her face heavily made up.)* Angustias!

ANGUSTIAS. Mother.

BERNARDA. You dare paint your face the day of your father's funeral!

ANGUSTIAS. He was not my father. My father died a long time ago. Have you forgotten?

BERNARDA. You owe more to this man, to your sisters' father, than to your own. Thanks to him, your fortune is increased.

ANGUSTIAS. We'll have to see about that.

BERNARDA. Out of decency. To show respect!

ANGUSTIAS. Let me go out, Mother.

BERNARDA. Go out?

MARIA JOSEFA. *(Offstage.)* Bernarda!

BERNARDA. After you have taken all this powder off your face. You ... you weakling! You painted whore!

MARIA JOSEFA. *(Offstage.)* Let me out, Bernarda!

BERNARDA. Exactly like your aunts! *(Bernarda violently removes the powder with her handkerchief.)*

PONCIA. Bernarda, don't be such a tyrant!

BERNARDA. My mother may be crazy but I still have my wits and I know exactly what I'm doing. *(They all enter.)*

MAGDALENA. What's going on?

BERNARDA. Nothing is "going on".

MAGDALENA. *(To Angustias.)* Well if you're arguing about the will — you're the richest — you can keep it all.

ANGUSTIAS. Keep your tongue where it belongs, in your purse.

BERNARDA. *(Beating on the floor.)* Do not think you can get the better of me. Until I am carried out of this house feet first, I will give the orders around here, for all of us! *(Voices are heard and Maria Josefa, Bernarda's mother, enters. She is very old and has decked out her head and breast with flowers.)*

MARIA JOSEFA.   Bernarda, where is my mantilla? Nothing I own will go to any of you. Not my rings, not my black moiré dress. Because none of you will ever get married. Not one of you! Bernarda, give me my pearl necklace.

BERNARDA.   *(To the Maid.)* Why did you let her in here?

MAID.   She got away from me.

MARIA JOSEFA.   Yes, I got away because I want to get married. I want to marry a real man from the shores of the sea, since all the men around here run away from women.

BERNARDA.   Silence, Mother.

MARIA JOSEFA.   No, I won't be silent. I don't want to look at these old maids burning to be married, turning their hearts to dust. I want to go home to my village, Bernarda. I want a man to get married to and be happy with.

BERNARDA.   Lock her up!

MARIA JOSEFA.   Let me go out, Bernarda! *(The Maid seizes Maria Josefa.)*

BERNARDA.   Help her, all of you! *(The daughters grab her.)*

MARIA JOSEFA.   I want to get away from here, Bernarda! Get married! By the shores of the sea! Down by the shores of the sea. Down by the shores of the sea. *(Quick curtain.)*

QUICK CURTAIN

END OF ACT ONE

ACT TWO

Bernarda's daughters are seated on low chairs, sewing. Magdalena is embroidering. La Poncia is with them.

ANGUSTIAS.   I cut the third sheet.

MARTIRIO.   That one goes to Amelia.

MAGDALENA.   Angustias, should I put Pepe's initials on that one, too?

ANGUSTIAS.   *(Dry.)* No.

MAGDALENA.   *(Calling, offstage to Adela.)* Adela, aren't you coming?

AMELIA.   She's probably stretched out on her bed.

PONCIA.   There's something wrong with that one. She's restless, shaky, she looks frightened — as if she had a lizard between her breasts.

MARTIRIO.   There's nothing more or less wrong with her than there is with the rest of us.

MAGDALENA.   All except Angustias.

ANGUSTIAS.   I feel fine, and anyone who doesn't like it can drop dead.

MAGDALENA.   *(Sarcastic.)* Let's admit it. Your best features are your figure and your tact.

ANGUSTIAS.   Fortunately I will soon be out of this hell.

MAGDALENA.   Maybe you won't get out.

MARTIRIO.   Stop it!

ANGUSTIAS.   Anyway, better to have gold in your purse than beautiful eyes in your face.

MAGDALENA.   This is going in one ear and out the other.

AMELIA.   I wish there were a breath of air.

MARTIRIO.   Last night, I couldn't sleep because of the heat.

AMELIA.   Me either.

MAGDALENA.   I got up to cool off. There was a dark storm cloud and a few drops of rain fell.

PONCIA.   At one o'clock in the morning, the heat was rising up out of the ground. I got up, too. Angustias was still with Pepe at the window.

MAGDALENA.   So late? What time did he go?

ANGUSTIAS. Magdalena, why ask if you saw him?

AMELIA. He left about half past one.

ANGUSTIAS. Oh yes? And how would you know?

AMELIA. I heard him cough and the sound of his horse's hooves.

PONCIA. But I felt he left about four.

ANGUSTIAS. It wasn't him.

PONCIA. I'm sure it was.

MARTIRIO. It seemed that way to me too.

MAGDALENA. Well, that's strange. *(Pause.)*

PONCIA. Angustias, come here, tell us, what did Pepe say to you the first time he came to your window?

ANGUSTIAS. Nothing. What should he have said? Just conversation.

MARTIRIO. It's very strange for two people who don't know each other to suddenly meet at a window and get engaged.

ANGUSTIAS. Well, I didn't find it strange.

AMELIA. I would have felt a little ... I don't know.

ANGUSTIAS. No, because, when a man comes to a window he already knows from all those people coming and going, going and coming, that she will say "Yes."

MARTIRIO. But he had to say it to you.

ANGUSTIAS. Well of course!

AMELIA. *(With curiosity.)* And how did he say it?

ANGUSTIAS. Well, it was nothing — just "You know I'm after you: I need a good woman, modest, and that's you if you're in agreement."

AMELIA. Those things embarrass me.

ANGUSTIAS. Me too, but you have to go through with them.

PONCIA. Did he say anything else?

ANGUSTIAS. Yes, he was the one who did all the talking.

MARTIRIO. And you?

ANGUSTIAS. I couldn't have. I felt as if my heart was coming out of my mouth. It was the first time I'd ever been alone at night with a man.

MAGDALENA. And such a handsome one at that!

ANGUSTIAS. He's not bad.

PONCIA. It's easier for people who've had a little experience, who've been taught how to speak and know what to say. When my husband, Evaristo the Birdman, first came to my window ... Hahaha.

MARTIRIO.   What happened?

PONCIA.   It was very dark. I saw him coming closer and when he arrived, he said to me: "Good evening." "Good evening," I said to him and we didn't speak for more than half an hour. The sweat was running down my entire body. And then Evaristo came closer and closer as if he was trying to squeeze through the bars and said in a very low voice, "Come here, I want to feel you!" *(They all laugh. Amelia gets up, runs and looks through the door.)*

AMELIA.   Ay, I thought Mother was coming!

MAGDALENA.   What she would have done to us! *(They go on laughing.)*

PONCIA.   And then after — he behaved himself. Instead of going to someone else, he started breeding canaries until he died. All of you are single, but you may as well know that fifteen days after the wedding, the man leaves the bed for the table and then the table for the tavern, and any woman who doesn't accept this, rots away crying in the corner.

AMELIA.   You didn't accept it.

PONCIA.   I could handle him.

MARTIRIO.   Is it true you hit him sometimes?

PONCIA.   I did: Once, I nearly put out one of his eyes.

MAGDALENA.   That's how women should be.

PONCIA.   I'm from the same school as your mother. One day, he said something or other to me — I can't remember what — and I killed all his canaries — with a hammer. *(They laugh.)*

MAGDALENA.   Oh, Adela, you shouldn't miss this!

AMELIA.   Adela! *(Pause.)*

MAGDALENA.   I'm going to go see. *(She goes out.)*

PONCIA.   That child is sick.

MARTIRIO.   Of course she is, she hardly sleeps.

PONCIA.   What *does* she do?

MARTIRIO.   How would I know what she does?

PONCIA.   You'd know better than me, since you sleep with just a wall between you.

ANGUSTIAS. Envy is eating her up.

AMELIA. Don't exaggerate.

ANGUSTIAS. I can see it in her eyes. She's getting to look like a madwoman.

MARTIRIO. Don't talk about madwomen here. This is the one place you shouldn't talk about that. *(Magdalena and Adela enter.)*

MAGDALENA. Didn't you say she was asleep?

ADELA. My whole body aches.

MARTIRIO. Didn't you sleep well last night?

ADELA. Yes.

MARTIRIO. *(With intention.)* Well then?

ADELA. *(With force.)* Leave me alone! Asleep or awake it's none of your business. It's my body and I'll do what I want with it.

MARTIRIO. I was concerned about you.

ADELA. Concerned, or nosy. Weren't you all sewing? Well, continue! I wish I was invisible so I could pass through a room without people asking me where I'm going all the time.

MAID. *(Entering.)* Bernarda's calling for you. The man with the lace is here. *(All but Adela and La Poncia go out, and as Martirio leaves, she looks fixedly at Adela.)*

ADELA. Stop looking at me. If you want, I'll give you my eyes, they're brighter than yours and my straight back to replace your hump. Just turn the other way when I go by!

PONCIA. Adela, she's your sister and the one who loves you the most.

ADELA. She follows me everywhere. She sneaks in my room sometimes to see if I'm sleeping. She won't let me breathe. And always: "What a shame about the face ... What a shame about the body ... it won't belong to anyone." But that's not going to happen. My body will belong to whoever I want.

PONCIA. *(With intention and in a low voice.)* To Pepe el Romano. Is that right?

ADELA. *(Startled.)* What did you say?

PONCIA. You heard, Adela.

ADELA. You shut your mouth!

PONCIA. *(In a loud voice.)* Do you think I haven't noticed?

ADELA. Lower your voice.

PONCIA. Kill those thoughts.

ADELA. What do you know about it?

PONCIA. We old women can see through walls. Where do you go when you get up at night?

ADELA. I wish you were blind!

PONCIA. When it's about what this is about, my head and both my hands are full of eyes. I want to know what you're planning. Why did you stand half-naked at the window with the light on the second night Pepe came to talk to your sister?

ADELA. That's not true!

PONCIA. Don't be a child. Leave your sister in peace! If you love Pepe el Romano, hold it in. *(Adela begins to cry.)* Besides, who says you can't marry him? Your sister Angustias is sickly. She won't survive her first birth. She's narrow in the hips, old, and in my experience I can tell you, she'll die. And then Pepe will do what many widowers around here do, he'll marry the youngest, and the prettiest, and that's you. Feed that hope, or forget about him, whatever you want, but don't go against the law of God!

ADELA. Shut your mouth!

PONCIA. I will not shut my mouth.

ADELA. Mind your own business. You sneak! Traitor!

PONCIA. I'll be your shadow.

ADELA. Instead of cleaning the house and going to bed to pray for your dead, you root around like an old sow drooling over other people's affairs.

PONCIA. I keep watch so people won't spit when they pass our door.

ADELA. Why have you suddenly developed this great affection for my sister?

PONCIA. I feel no affection for any of you. But I want to live in a decent house. I don't want to be disgraced in my old age.

ADELA. Your advice is useless. It's too late. I wouldn't just walk over you, you're only a servant, I'd walk over my mother to put out the fire that's running through my legs and burning in my mouth. What could you say about me? That I lock myself in my room and don't open the door? That I don't sleep? I'm quicker than you. See if you can catch the rabbit with your bare hands.

PONCIA. Don't defy me Adela, don't you defy me. Because I can shout, light the lamps, and make the bells ring.

ADELA. You can mount four thousand bright yellow flares on the walls of this house. No one can stop what has to happen.

PONCIA. You want that man so much?

ADELA. So much! When I look into his eyes it's like I am slowly drinking his blood.

PONCIA. I can't hear you.

ADELA. Oh, but you'll have to. I used to be afraid of you. But I'm stronger than you now. *(Angustias enters.)*

ANGUSTIAS. Always arguing.

PONCIA. Of course. She wants me, in all this heat, to go and get her I don't know what from the store.

ANGUSTIAS. Did you get me that perfume?

PONCIA. The most expensive one and the face powder. I put them on the table in your room. *(Angustias goes out.)*

ADELA. And keep it shut!

PONCIA. We'll see. *(Magdalena, Martirio and Amelia enter.)*

MAGDALENA. Did you see the lace?

AMELIA. The pieces for Angustias' wedding sheets are beautiful.

ADELA. *(To Martirio, who is carrying some lace.)* And these?

MARTIRIO. Mine, for a nightgown.

ADELA. Well, it takes a sense of humor.

MARTIRIO. For me to look at. I don't have to flaunt myself in front of anyone.

PONCIA. Nobody sees you in a nightgown.

MARTIRIO. *(With intention, looking at Adela.)* Sometimes ... But I love underclothes. If I was rich I'd have it all made from Dutch linen, all imported from Holland. It's one of the few pleasures I've got.

PONCIA. This lace would be nice for babies' caps and christening gowns. I couldn't afford it for mine. Maybe Angustias will use it for hers. When she starts having babies, you'll be sewing morning and night.

MAGDALENA. I don't plan to sew a stitch.

AMELIA. Much less take care of someone else's children.

Look at how our neighbors sacrifice themselves for those four little brats.

PONCIA.   They're better off than you. At least they laugh and you can hear them fighting.

MARTIRIO.   Go and work for them.

PONCIA.   No. Fate has sent me to this convent. *(The bells are heard.)*

MAGDALENA.   That's the men going back to work.

PONCIA.   It's three o'clock.

MARTIRIO.   In this heat!

ADELA.   *(Sitting down.)* Ay. If only we could go to the fields too!

MAGDALENA.   *(Sitting down.)* Each class has its own work.

MARTIRIO.   *(Sitting down.)* That's how it is.

AMELIA.   *(Sitting down.)* Ay!

PONCIA.   There's nothing like being in the fields this time of year. The reapers arrived yesterday morning. Forty or fifty handsome young men.

MAGDALENA.   Where are they from this year?

PONCIA.   From far, far away. From the mountains. Happy! Like poplar trees! Shouting and throwing stones! Last night a woman arrived dressed in spangles and danced to an accordion. Fifteen of them paid her to go to the olive grove with them. I watched — from far off. The one who made the deal was a young man with green eyes, hard and tightly packed as a sheaf of wheat.

AMELIA.   Really?

ADELA.   It's possible.

PONCIA.   A few years ago another of these women came to the village and I gave my oldest son the money myself so he could go with her. Men need these things.

ADELA.   They're forgiven everything.

AMELIA.   To be born a woman is the worst punishment.

MAGDALENA.   Not even our eyes belong to us. *(A distant song is heard, coming nearer.)*

PONCIA.   Here they come. *(Tambourines and carranacas are heard. Pause. They all listen in the silence cut by the sun.)*

REAPERS.

Here come the reapers
In search of the grain
Reaping the hearts
Of the women they claim.

MARTIRIO.   They don't care about the blazing sun!

ADELA.   I wish I was a reaper, to come and go as I please. Then I could forget what's eating us alive.

MARTIRIO.   What do you have to forget?

ADELA.   Everyone has something.

MARTIRIO.   *(Profoundly.)* Everyone. *(The song grows more distant.)*

PONCIA.   Quiet! Quiet!

REAPERS.

Open your doors and your windows
You women that live in this town
The reaper asks for roses
To decorate his crown.

(Martirio sings with it, nostalgically. Adela with passion finishes it. The song gets further away.)

PONCIA.   They're turning the corner.

ADELA.   Let's watch from the window in my room.

PONCIA.   Be careful not to open the shutters too wide: They like to give them a push to see who's looking. *(The three leave. Martirio is left sitting on the low chair with her head between her hands.)*

AMELIA.   *(Drawing near her.)* What's wrong with you?

MARTIRIO.   The heat is making me sick.

AMELIA.   Is that all?

MARTIRIO.   I wish November would come, the rainy days, the frost, anything but this endless summer.

AMELIA.   The summer will pass and it will come again.

MARTIRIO.   Well of course. *(Pause.)* What time did you go to sleep last night?

AMELIA.   I don't know. I sleep like a log. Why?

MARTIRIO.   Nothing. But I thought I heard people in the corral.

AMELIA. Oh?

MARTIRIO. Very late.

AMELIA. And you weren't scared?

MARTIRIO. No. I've heard it other nights.

AMELIA. We should be careful. Couldn't it have been the farmhands?

MARTIRIO. The farmhands come at six.

AMELIA. Maybe a young, unbroken mule.

MARTIRIO. *(Between her teeth.)* Yes, that's it, a young, unbroken, mule.

AMELIA. We should all keep watch.

MARTIRIO. No, no don't say anything. Maybe I imagined it.

AMELIA. Maybe. *(Pause. Amelia starts to go.)*

MARTIRIO. Amelia!

AMELIA. *(At the door.)* What? *(Pause.)*

MARTIRIO. Nothing. *(Pause.)*

AMELIA. Why did you call me? *(Pause.)*

MARTIRIO. It just came out. I wasn't thinking. *(Pause.)*

AMELIA. Go and lie down for a while.

ANGUSTIAS. *(Bursts in furiously, in a manner that makes a great contrast with previous quiet scene.)* Where is the picture of Pepe I had under my pillow? Which one of you took it?

MARTIRIO. No one.

AMELIA. It's not like he's Saint Bartholomew. *(Poncia, Magdalena and Adela enter.)*

ANGUSTIAS. Where is the picture?

ADELA. What picture?

ANGUSTIAS. The picture of Pepe, one of you has hidden it from me.

MAGDALENA. You have the audacity to say that?

ANGUSTIAS. It was in my room and it's not there now!

MARTIRIO. Couldn't it have slipped out into the corral in the middle of the night? Pepe likes to walk in the moonlight.

ANGUSTIAS. Don't play games with me! When he comes I'll tell him!

PONCIA. *(Looking at Adela.)* No, don't do that. It'll turn up.

ANGUSTIAS. I would like to know which one of you has it?

ADELA. *(Looking at Martirio.)* Well somebody — everybody

does, but not me.

MARTIRIO. *(With meaning.)* Naturally, never you.

BERNARDA. *(Entering, with her cane.)* What is this commotion in my house? In the silence of the heat of the day? The neighbors will have their ears glued to the walls.

ANGUSTIAS. They've taken the picture of my fiancé.

BERNARDA. Who? Who?

ANGUSTIAS. Them!

BERNARDA. Which of you? *(Silence.)* Answer me! *(Silence. To Poncia.)* Search their rooms: Look in the beds. *(To Daughters.)* This comes from giving you too long a leash. But I'll haunt your dreams. *(To Angustias.)* Are you sure?

ANGUSTIAS. Yes.

BERNARDA. You looked carefully?

ANGUSTIAS. Yes, mother. *(They all stand around in embarrassed silence.)*

BERNARDA. At the end of my life you force me to drink the most bitter poison a mother can bear. *(To Poncia.)* You didn't find it? *(Poncia enters.)*

PONCIA. Here it is.

BERNARDA. Where was it?

PONCIA. It ... was ...

BERNARDA. Don't be afraid to say it.

PONCIA. *(In a surprised manner.)* ... In between the sheets of Martirio's bed.

BERNARDA. *(To Martirio.)* Is this true?

MARTIRIO. It's true. *(Advancing on her, beating her with her cane.)*

BERNARDA. I'd like to squash you like an insect under my foot! You scorpion, you snake-in-the-grass!

MARTIRIO. *(Furious, using the formal.)* Don't you hit me, Mother!

BERNARDA. I'll hit you all I want!

MARTIRIO. If I let you. You hear me? Get away from me!

PONCIA. Don't be disrespectful to your mother.

ANGUSTIAS. *(Holding Bernarda.)* Leave her alone. Please.

BERNARDA. Not even a tear.

MARTIRIO. I'm not going to cry to please you!

BERNARDA. Why did you take the picture?

MARTIRIO. Can't I play a joke on my own sister? Why else would I want it?

ADELA. *(Leaping forward, full of jealousy.)* It wasn't a joke, you never liked playing games. It was something else, bursting to come out. Say it!

MARTIRIO. You be quiet, and don't you make me speak, because if I do, the walls will fold in on each other for shame!

ADELA. A wicked tongue never stops inventing lies.

BERNARDA. Adela!

MAGDALENA. You're both mad.

AMELIA. And you torture us with your shameful thoughts.

MARTIRIO. Some people do shameful things.

ADELA. Until they strip naked and the river sweeps them away.

BERNARDA. You are *perverse!*

ANGUSTIAS. It's not my fault Pepe el Romano chose me.

ADELA. For your money.

ANGUSTIAS. Mother!

MARTIRIO. For your fields and your orchards.

BERNARDA. Silence!

MAGDALENA. It's the truth.

BERNARDA. Silence, I said! I could see the storm brewing, but I didn't think it would break so soon. Oh, you've laid a heavy stone of hatred on my heart. But I'm not old yet, and I'll chain up the five of you in this house my father built, so not even the weeds in the yard will know of my anguish. Get out! All of you! *(They go out. Bernarda sits down desolately. La Poncia is standing close to the wall. Bernarda recovers herself, and beats on the floor.)* Use a firm hand Bernarda, remember, you have obligations.

PONCIA. May I speak?

BERNARDA. Speak. I'm sorry you heard that. It's never wise to have an outsider in a family.

PONCIA. What I've seen, I've seen.

BERNARDA. Angustias must get married right away.

PONCIA. Of course. We'll have to get her away from here.

BERNARDA. Not her. Him!

PONCIA.   Of course. He's the one to get away from here — good thinking.

BERNARDA.   I don't think. There are things one cannot and should not think. I give orders.

PONCIA.   Do you think he'll want to go away?

BERNARDA.   *(Rising.)* What do you mean?

PONCIA.   He will of course be marrying Angustias.

BERNARDA.   Speak up! I know you well enough to know when you've got your knife out for me.

PONCIA.   I never knew a warning could be called murder.

BERNARDA.   You have a warning for me?

PONCIA.   Bernarda, I'm not making accusations, I'm just saying open your eyes, and you'll see.

BERNARDA.   See what?

PONCIA.   You've always been smart. You can spot the worst in other people from a hundred miles away: Sometimes I think you can read their thoughts. But one's children are one's children. Now you're being blind.

BERNARDA.   Are you talking about Martirio ...

PONCIA.   All right, Martirio. *(With curiosity.)* I wonder why she took that picture.

BERNARDA.   *(Shielding her daughter.)* She says it was a joke. What else could it be?

PONCIA.   *(With energy.)* Do you really believe that?

BERNARDA.   Yes!

PONCIA.   All right, we are talking about your own. But what if we were talking about the neighbors from across the way?

BERNARDA.   Now you're starting to sharpen the knife.

PONCIA.   Bernarda, something very wrong is going on here. I don't want to put the blame on you, but you've never given your daughters any freedom. Martirio is sick for love, I don't care what you say. Why didn't you let her marry Enrique Humanes? Why, on the day he was to come to her window, why did you send him word not to come?

BERNARDA.   And I'd do it a thousand times over! My blood will not mix with the blood of the Humanes as long as I live! His father was a farmhand!

PONCIA.   Look what's come of putting on airs.

BERNARDA.   I put them on because I can afford to, and you cannot, because you know what you come from.

PONCIA.   *(With hatred.)* Don't remind me. I'm an old woman. I've always been grateful for your protection.

BERNARDA.   You don't show it.

PONCIA.   *(With hate masked by sweetness.)* Martirio will forget about this.

BERNARDA.   And if she doesn't forget, so much the worse for her. I don't think something "very wrong" is going on here. That's what you'd like to believe. And if one day something should happen, you can be sure it won't get beyond these walls.

PONCIA.   I wouldn't be too sure of that. There are other people in this village who can read thoughts at a distance.

BERNARDA.   How you would love to see me and my daughters on our way to the whorehouse!

PONCIA.   No one knows their own end.

BERNARDA.   I know mine! And my daughters! The whorehouse was for a certain woman now dead.

PONCIA.   *(Furious.)* Bernarda, respect the memory of my mother.

BERNARDA.   Then stop plaguing me with your wicked thoughts! *(Pause.)*

PONCIA.   Better if I stay out of everything.

BERNARDA.   That's right. Work. Keep your mouth shut. The duty of all who work for hire.

PONCIA.   I can't do that. Don't you think it would be better if Pepe were married to Martirio or ... yes! or to Adela?

BERNARDA.   No, I don't think.

PONCIA.   *(With meaning.)* Adela. Now there's the true bride for el Romano.

BERNARDA.   Things are never the way we'd like them to be.

PONCIA.   No, but it's hard work turning them from their true course. For Pepe to be with Angustias seems wrong to me — and to other people as well. And even to the wind. Who can tell if things will turn out as they should?

BERNARDA.   Here you go again...! Sneaking up on me. My daughters respect me, and they have never gone against my will.

PONCIA. That's right! But the minute they break free, they'll climb to the rooftops.

BERNARDA. Then I'll throw stones at them to bring them down.

PONCIA. You were always the bravest.

BERNARDA. I've always enjoyed a good fight.

PONCIA. Isn't it strange? You should see the fever Angustias is in over her lover. At her age! And it seems he's smitten, too. Yesterday, my oldest son told me that when he passed by with the oxen at four-thirty in the morning, they were still there talking at the window.

BERNARDA. At four-thirty?

ANGUSTIAS. *(Entering.)* That's a lie!

PONCIA. That's what he told me.

BERNARDA. *(To Angustias.)* Talk.

ANGUSTIAS. For over a week Pepe has been leaving at one o'clock. May God strike me dead if I'm lying.

MARTIRIO. *(Entering.)* I heard him leave at four too.

BERNARDA. Did you see him with your own eyes?

MARTIRIO. I didn't want to be seen. Don't you go to the side window to talk now?

ANGUSTIAS. We talk at my bedroom window. *(Adela appears at the door.)*

MARTIRIO. Then . . .

BERNARDA. What is going on in this house?

PONCIA. Careful or you'll find out. All I know is that Pepe was at one of your windows — at half past four in the morning.

BERNARDA. Are you sure?

PONCIA. You can't be sure of anything in this life.

ADELA. Mother, don't listen to her, she wants to ruin us all.

BERNARDA. I know how to find out. If people in this town want to spread lies about me, they'll find they've run into a stone wall. No one is to talk about this! or waves of filth could drown us all.

MARTIRIO. I don't like to lie.

PONCIA. Then something is going to happen.

BERNARDA. Nothing is going to happen. I was born to keep my eyes open and I won't shut them now until the day I die.

ANGUSTIAS.   I have the right to know.

BERNARDA.   You have the right to nothing except to do what I tell you. No one tells me what I can or can not do. *(To Poncia.)* You put your own house in order. Nothing happens here without my knowing about it.

MAID.   *(Entering.)* There's a big crowd at the top of the street and all the neighbors are at their doors.

BERNARDA.   *(To Poncia.)* You, run and see what's going on. *(The girls are about to run out.)* Where do you think you're going? You women, staring at doorways, breaking your mourning. Go to your rooms, all of you! *(They go out. Bernarda leaves. Distant shouts are heard. Martirio and Adela enter and listen, not daring to step further than the front door.)*

MARTIRIO.   You're lucky I didn't open my mouth.

ADELA.   I could have said something, too.

MARTIRIO.   What could you have said? You won't go on like this much longer.

ADELA.   I'll have it all.

MARTIRIO.   I'll tear you out of his arms.

ADELA.   Martirio, leave me alone.

MARTIRIO.   None of us will have him!

ADELA.   He wants to live with me.

MARTIRIO.   I saw how he was holding you.

ADELA.   I didn't want this. It's as if I'm being dragged by a rope.

MARTIRIO.   I'll see you dead first. *(Magdalena and Angustias look in. The tumult is increasing. Poncia enters with Bernarda from another door.)*

PONCIA.   Bernarda!

BERNARDA.   What is going on?

PONCIA.   It's Librada's daughter, the unmarried one, had a baby, and nobody knows whose it is.

ADELA.   A baby?

PONCIA.   And to hide her shame, she killed it and buried it under the rocks, but some dogs dug it up and left it at her door. Now they want to kill her. They're dragging her through the streets.

BERNARDA.   Good, let them come, let them bring olive

34

switches and pick handles. Let them come and kill her.

ADELA.   No! No! Not kill her!

MARTIRIO.   Yes — let us go out there too!

BERNARDA.   Any woman who tramples on her decency must pay for it. *(Outside a woman's shriek and a great clamor is heard.)*

ADELA.   Let her escape! Don't go out there!

MARTIRIO.   *(Looking at Adela.)* Let her pay what she owes!

BERNARDA.   *(At the archway.)* Finish her off before the police get here. Fiery coals in the place where she sinned.

ADELA.   *(Holding her belly.)* No! No!

BERNARDA.   Kill her! Kill her!

BERNARDA and MARTIRIO.   Kill her! Kill her! Kill her!

CURTAIN

END OF ACT TWO

ACT THREE

It is night. The doorways, illuminated by the lights inside the rooms, give a glow to the stage. At Center there is a table with a shaded oil lamp around which Bernarda and her Daughters are eating. La Poncia serves them. Prudencia sits apart. When the curtain rises, there is a great silence interrupted only by the noise of plates and silverware.

PRUDENCIA. *(She rises.)* I'm going, Bernarda. It's been a long visit.

BERNARDA. Wait, Prudencia. We never see each other.

PRUDENCIA. Have they sounded the last bell for the rosary?

PONCIA. Not yet. *(Prudencia sits down again.)*

BERNARDA. And your husband, how is he?

PRUDENCIA. The same.

BERNARDA. We never see him either.

PRUDENCIA. You know how he is. Ever since he fought his brothers over the inheritance he won't use the front door. He puts up a ladder and climbs over the back wall.

BERNARDA. A real man! And your daughter?

PRUDENCIA. He has never forgiven her.

BERNARDA. He's right.

PRUDENCIA. I don't know about that.

BERNARDA. A daughter who disobeys stops being a daughter and becomes an enemy.

PRUDENCIA. I let water run. *(A heavy blow is heard against the walls.)* What was that?

BERNARDA. The stallion. He's tied in his stall and he's kicking against the wall. *(Shouting.)* Tether him and take him out in the yard! *(In a lower voice.)* He must be too hot.

PRUDENCIA. Are you going to put him to the new mares?

BERNARDA. At daylight.

PRUDENCIA. You've known how to increase your stock.

BERNARDA. Through a lot of money and hard work.

PONCIA. *(Interrupting.)* She has the best herd in this part of

36

the country. It's too bad the prices are down.

BERNARDA. Do you want some cheese, or some honey?

PRUDENCIA. I have no appetite. *(The blow is heard again.)*

PONCIA. Oh for God's sake!

PRUDENCIA. I can feel it right through my chest.

BERNARDA. *(Rising, furiously.)* Do I have to say everything twice? Let him out to roll in the straw! *(Pause. Then, as though speaking to the Stableman.)* Tether the mares in the corral, but let him run free, or he'll kick the walls down. *(She returns to the table and sits again.)* Ay! What a life!

PRUDENCIA. You have to fight like a man.

BERNARDA. That's it. *(Adela gets up from the table.)* Where are you going?

ADELA. For a drink of water.

BERNARDA. *(Raising her voice.)* Bring a pitcher of fresh water. *(To Adela.)* You can sit down. *(Adela sits down.)*

PRUDENCIA. And Angustias, when will she be married?

BERNARDA. They come to ask for her in three days.

PRUDENCIA. You must be happy.

BERNARDA. *(Pause.)* Angustias.

ANGUSTIAS. Of course.

AMELIA. *(To Magdalena.)* You spilled the salt!

MAGDALENA. You can't have worse luck than you're already having.

AMELIA. It's always a bad sign.

BERNARDA. That's enough.

PRUDENCIA. *(To Angustias.)* Has he given you the ring yet?

ANGUSTIAS. See? *(She holds it out.)*

PRUDENCIA. It's beautiful. Three pearls. In my day, pearls meant tears.

ANGUSTIAS. Well, things have changed.

ADELA. Things don't change their meaning. Engagement rings should be diamonds.

PRUDENCIA. The most appropriate.

BERNARDA. With or without pearls, life is what you make it.

MARTIRIO. Or what God makes for you.

PRUDENCIA. I've been told your furniture is beautiful.

BERNARDA. It ought to be. I spent 16,000 *reales*.

PRUDENCIA. What's important is everything is for the best.

ADELA. And you never know.

BERNARDA. There's no reason why it shouldn't be. *(Bells are heard very distantly.)*

PRUDENCIA. The last bell. *(To Angustias.)* I'll come back soon and you can show me the dress.

ANGUSTIAS. Whenever you like.

PRUDENCIA. Good night. God be with you.

BERNARDA. Good-bye, Prudencia.

ALL FIVE DAUGHTERS. *(At the same time.)* God be with you. *(Pause. Prudencia goes out.)*

BERNARDA. Well, we've eaten. That's done. *(They rise.)*

ADELA. I'm going to walk to the front gate and stretch my legs. *(Magdalena sits down in a low chair and leans against the wall.)*

AMELIA. I'll go with you.

MARTIRIO. Me too.

ADELA. *(With contained hate.)* I won't get lost.

AMELIA. You should have company at night. *(They go out. Bernarda sits down. Angustias is clearing the table.)*

BERNARDA. I told you once already! I want you to speak with your sister Martirio. What happened with the picture was a joke and you should forget about it.

ANGUSTIAS. You know she hates me.

BERNARDA. Each of us knows what we think inside. I don't pry into people's hearts, but I do insist you keep up appearances and we have peace in the family. Understood?

ANGUSTIAS. Yes.

BERNARDA. Then that's settled.

MAGDALENA. *(She is almost asleep.)* Anyway, you're going to be leaving soon ... *(She falls asleep.)*

ANGUSTIAS. Not soon enough for me.

BERNARDA. What time did you finish talking last night?

ANGUSTIAS. At half past twelve.

BERNARDA. What does Pepe talk about?

ANGUSTIAS. He's distracted. He always talks to me as if he was thinking of something else. When I ask him what's wrong, he says, "We men have our worries."

38

BERNARDA. Then don't ask him. Especially once you are married. Speak if he speaks, look at him when he looks at you. That way you'll get along.

ANGUSTIAS. Mother, I think he's hiding a lot of things from me.

BERNARDA. Don't try and find out what they are. Don't ask him, and above all never let him see you cry.

ANGUSTIAS. I should be happy, and I'm not.

BERNARDA. It's all the same.

ANGUSTIAS. Some nights I stare at him through the window bars, and he seems to fade away, like he's being covered by a cloud of dust kicked up by the sheep.

BERNARDA. It's because you're not strong.

ANGUSTIAS. I hope it's that.

BERNARDA. Is he coming tonight?

ANGUSTIAS. No. He went to the city with his mother.

BERNARDA. Then we'll get to bed early. Magdalena?

ANGUSTIAS. She's asleep. *(Adela, Martirio and Amelia enter.)*

AMELIA. It's such a dark night!

ADELA. You can't see two steps in front of you.

MARTIRIO. A good night for thieves, or anybody who needs to hide.

ADELA. The stallion was in the middle of the corral. White! Looking twice as big as usual! He filled up the darkness.

AMELIA. It looked like a ghost.

ADELA. There are stars in the sky as big as fists.

MARTIRIO. *(About Adela.)* This one was staring at them until she almost broke her neck.

ADELA. Don't you like them?

MARTIRIO. I don't care what goes on above the rooftops. I have enough to handle with what goes on down here.

ADELA. Well, that's the way it is for you.

BERNARDA. It's the same for you as it is for her.

ANGUSTIAS. Good night.

ADELA. Are you going to bed now?

ANGUSTIAS. Yes. Pepe isn't coming tonight. *(Angustias exits.)*

ADELA. Mother, why do people cross themselves every time there's a shooting star or a flash of lightning?

BERNARDA. Oh, the old people know lots of things we've forgotten.

AMELIA. I close my eyes so I won't see them.

ADELA. Not me. I like to see what's been quiet for years and years suddenly shoot fire.

MARTIRIO. All that has nothing to do with us.

BERNARDA. Best not to think about them.

ADELA. Oh what a beautiful night! I'd like to stay up and feel the cool breeze from the fields.

BERNARDA. But we have to go to bed. Magdalena!

AMELIA. She's asleep.

BERNARDA. Magdalena!

MAGDALENA. Leave me alone.

BERNARDA. Go to bed!

MAGDALENA. *(Rising, in a bad humor.)* You don't give anyone a moment's peace. *(She goes off grumbling.)*

AMELIA. Good night. *(She goes out.)*

BERNARDA. You two off to bed too.

MARTIRIO. Why isn't Angustias's fiancé coming tonight?

BERNARDA. He went on a trip.

MARTIRIO. *(Looking at Adela.)* Ah!

ADELA. Good night. *(She goes out. Martirio drinks some water and goes out slowly, looking at the door to the yard. La Poncia enters.)*

PONCIA. Are you still here?

BERNARDA. I'm enjoying the quiet and unable to see the "something very wrong" that is "going on" here, according to you.

PONCIA. Bernarda, let's not go any further with this.

BERNARDA. In this house there's one way of doing things. My watchfulness takes care of everything.

PONCIA. Nothing is going on outwardly. That's true. But your daughters live as if they were locked up in a cupboard. Neither you nor anyone else can see into their hearts.

BERNARDA. My daughters' hearts beat calmly enough.

PONCIA. That's your business. You're their mother. I have enough to do looking after your house.

BERNARDA. Yes. Now you've turned quiet.

PONCIA. I keep my place — that's all.

BERNARDA. Your problem is you have nothing to say. If there were weeds growing in this house, you'd make sure all the sheep in the neighborhood came here to graze.

PONCIA. I hide more than you think.

BERNARDA. Do your sons still see Pepe here at four in the morning? Do they still spread the same malicious gossip about this house?

PONCIA. They say nothing.

BERNARDA. Because there's nothing they can say. No meat to sink their teeth into, thanks to my vigilance.

PONCIA. Bernarda, I don't want to talk about this because I'm afraid of what you'll do. But don't be too sure.

BERNARDA. Oh, but I am. Very sure.

PONCIA. Lightning could strike. A rush of blood could suddenly stop your heart.

BERNARDA. Nothing will happen here. I'm on guard now against all your suspicions.

PONCIA. All the better for you.

BERNARDA. *(She rises.)* Exactly. *(The Maid enters.)*

MAID. I've just finished the dishes. Is there anything else, Bernarda?

BERNARDA. Nothing. I'm going to get some rest.

PONCIA. What time do you want me to wake you?

BERNARDA. Don't. I intend to sleep soundly tonight. *(She goes out.)*

PONCIA. When you are powerless against the sea, it's better to turn your back on it so you don't see it.

MAID. She's so proud, she puts a blindfold on herself.

PONCIA. Well, there's nothing I can do. I tried to put a stop to this, but now — it frightens me too much. Feel the silence? In every room, a storm is brewing, and the day it breaks it'll sweep us all away. I said what I had to say.

MAID. Bernarda thinks nothing can stand against her. She doesn't know the power of a man among women alone.

PONCIA. It's not all Pepe el Romano's fault. It's true last year he chased after Adela and she was crazy about him, but Adela should have kept her place and not led him on. A man is a man.

41

MAID. Some say he's talked to Adela many nights.

PONCIA. It's true. *(Whispers.)* And that's not all.

MAID. Bernarda's rushing the wedding: Maybe nothing will happen.

PONCIA. No, things have gone too far already. Adela's made up her mind, whatever happens, and the others constantly keep watch.

MAID. Martirio, too?

PONCIA. That one's the worst. She's a pool of poison. She knows she can't get el Romano herself, and she'd drown the whole world if it was in her power.

MAID. They're bad!

PONCIA. They're women without men, that's all. In matters like these you even forget your own blood. Sssshh! *(She listens.)*

MAID. What is it?

PONCIA. The dogs are barking.

MAID. Someone must have passed by the front door. *(Adela enters wearing a white petticoat and a corselet.)*

PONCIA. Didn't you go to bed?

ADELA. I'm getting a drink of water. *(She drinks from a glass on the table.)*

PONCIA. I thought you were asleep.

ADELA. I got thirsty. What about you, don't you ever rest?

MAID. Soon now. *(Adela goes out.)*

PONCIA. Let's go.

MAID. We've earned some sleep. Bernarda doesn't let me rest the whole day.

PONCIA. Take the lamp.

MAID. The dogs are going mad.

PONCIA. They're not going to let us sleep. *(They go out. The stage is left almost dark. Maria Josefa enters with a lamb in her arms.)*

MARIA JOSEFA. *(Singing.)*

Little lamb, child of mine
Let's go to the shore of the sea
The little ant is at his door
I'll give you my breast and bread
Bernarda
Face of a leopard

Magdalena
Of a hyena
Little lamb
Baa! Baa! Baa!
We'll go to the palms at Bethlehem's gate
You and I won't want to sleep
A door will open on its own
On the beach you and I
will hide in a hut of coral reef.
Bernarda
Face of a leopard
Magdalena
Of a hyena
Little lamb, baaa, baaa
We'll go to the palms at Bethlehem's gate.
(Adela enters and runs to the corral door as Maria Josefa pounds on the front door. Martirio enters.)
MARTIRIO.   Grandmother, where are you going?
MARIA JOSEFA.   Have you come to open the door for me? Who are you?
MARTIRIO.   How did you get out here?
MARIA JOSEFA.   I escaped. Which one are you?
MARTIRIO.   Go back to bed.
MARIA JOSEFA.   Oh, now I see you. Martirio, face of a martyr. And when are you going to have a baby? I've had this one.
MARTIRIO.   Where did you get that lamb?
MARIA JOSEFA.   I know it's a lamb. But why can't a lamb be a baby? It's better to have a lamb than to have nothing. Bernarda, face of a leopard. Magdalena, of a hyena.
MARTIRIO.   Don't shout.
MARIA JOSEFA.   It's true. Everything is dark. Because my hair is white you think I can't have babies. Babies and babies and babies. This baby will have white hair, and will have another baby and all with white hair, like snow. We'll be like the waves, one after another. And then we'll sit down and we'll all have white heads and we'll be the foam of the sea. Why isn't there any foam here? Nothing but mourning shawls.
MARTIRIO.   Shh, Shh.

MARIA JOSEFA. When my neighbor had a baby, I took her some chocolate, and later, she brought me some — always and always and always. You'll have white hair, but your neighbors won't come. I have to go now, but I'm afraid the dogs may bite me. Will you come with me out to the fields? I don't like the fields. I like houses, but open houses with the women stretched out on their beds with their little children, and the men outside sitting on their chairs. Pepe el Romano is a giant! Every one of you loves him. But he'll devour you because you're all just grains of wheat. No, not grains of wheat. Frogs without tongues.

MARTIRIO. Go to bed. *(She pushes her.)*

MARIA JOSEFA. Yes. But later you'll open the door for me. Won't you?

MARTIRIO. Of course.

MARIA JOSEFA. *(Weeping. Sings her lullaby.)*

  Ah, little lamb, child of mine
  Let's go to the shore of the sea
  The little ant will be at his door
  I'll give you my breast and bread.

(She goes. Martirio closes the door on Maria Josefa, locks it and goes to the yard door. There she hesitates, but goes two steps further.)

MARTIRIO. *(Low voice.)* Adela. *(Pause. Louder.)* Adela! *(Adela enters. Her hair is disarranged.)*

ADELA. Why are you looking for me?

MARTIRIO. Stay away from that man!

ADELA. Who are you to tell me?

MARTIRIO. That's no place for a decent woman.

ADELA. How you would love to take my place!

MARTIRIO. *(Louder.)* This can't continue.

ADELA. This is only the beginning. I have the strength to do it, and the spirit, and the looks, which you don't have. I saw death under this roof and I went out to look for what is mine, for what belongs to me.

MARTIRIO. That man without a soul, came here for another woman. You put yourself between them.

ADELA. He came for the money, but his eyes were always on me.

MARTIRIO.   I won't let you steal him. He will marry Angustias.

ADELA.   You know he doesn't love her.

MARTIRIO.   I know that.

ADELA.   You know because you've seen — he loves me!

MARTIRIO.   *(Despairing.)* Yes!

ADELA.   *(Coming closer to her.)* He loves me! He loves me!

MARTIRIO.   Stick me with a knife if you want, just don't say that again!

ADELA.   That's why you're trying to stop me from going away with him. It makes no difference to you if he's putting his arms around someone he doesn't love: I don't care either. He could spend a hundred years with Angustias, but if he's holding me, caressing me, you can't stand it because you're in love with him too. You love him!

MARTIRIO.   Yes! Let me say it without shame! Yes! My heart is bursting with envy. I love him!

ADELA.   *(Impulsively, hugging her.)* Martirio, Martirio, it's not my fault.

MARTIRIO.   Don't touch me! My blood isn't yours anymore. No matter how much I want to see you as a sister, I can only see you as another woman. *(She pushes her away.)*

ADELA.   Then there's no way out. Whoever has to drown will drown. Pepe el Romano is mine. He will carry me away to the reeds by the sea.

MARTIRIO.   He will not.

ADELA.   I can't stand the horror of being under this roof anymore, not after tasting his mouth. I will be what he wants me to be. All the village against me, burning me with their pointing fingers, persecuted by those who call themselves decent people, and I will put on, in front of them all, the crown of thorns that belongs to the mistresses of married men.

MARTIRIO.   Be quiet!

ADELA.   Yes, we'll let him marry Angustias, it's not important to me, but I'll move to a little house by myself, where he'll come and see me whenever he wants, whenever he desires me.

MARTIRIO.   Not if there's a drop of blood in my body.

ADELA.   You can't stop me. You're weak. I could bring a wild stallion to its knees with the strength of my little finger.

MARTIRIO.   Don't you raise your voice at me, I can't stand it. My heart is full of a force so vicious, I can't stop it from drowning me.

ADELA.   They teach us to love our sisters. God must have abandoned me in this darkness, because I see you now as if I'd never seen you anywhere before. *(A whistle is heard at the front door and Adela runs toward the door, but Martirio gets in front of her.)*

MARTIRIO.   Where are you going?

ADELA.   Move away from that door!

MARTIRIO.   Get by me if you can!

ADELA.   Get away! *(They struggle.)*

MARTIRIO.   *(Shouts.)* Mother! Mother!

ADELA.   Let me go! *(Bernarda enters. She wears petticoats and a black shawl.)*

BERNARDA.   Stop this! Oh, how I wish I could make lightning strike.

MARTIRIO.   *(Pointing to Adela.)* She was with him! Look at her, she's covered with straw!

BERNARDA.   *(Going furiously toward Adela.)* The bed of a whore.

ADELA.   *(Facing her.)* Here ends my imprisonment! *(She snatches her mother's cane and breaks it in two.)* That's what I do with the warden's rod. Do not take another step! No one gives me orders here except Pepe!

MAGDALENA.   *(Entering.)* Adela! *(Poncia and Angustias enter.)*

ADELA.   I belong to him! *(To Angustias.)* Accept it. He will be master of this house. Go out in the yard and tell him. He's out there now, panting like a lion.

ANGUSTIAS.   My God!

BERNARDA.   The gun, where is the gun! *(Bernarda rushes out. Martirio exits behind her. Amelia enters and looks on frightened, leaning her head against the wall. Adela tries to run out.)*

ANGUSTIAS.   *(Holding her.)* You're not leaving here, to triumph with your body! You thief! You shame our house!

MAGDALENA.   Let her go where we never have to see her again! *(A shot is heard.)*

BERNARDA.   *(Entering.)* Find him now, if you dare.

MARTIRIO.   *(Entering.)* That's the end of it.

ADELA. Pe-pe! My God! Pepe! *(She runs out.)*
PONCIA. Did you kill him?
MARTIRIO. No. He galloped away on his horse.
BERNARDA. It was my fault. A woman can't aim.
MAGDALENA. Then why did you say...?
MARTIRIO. For her! I'd like to pour a river of blood over her.
PONCIA. Damn you!
MAGDALENA. You devil!
BERNARDA. It's better this way. *(A thud is heard.)* Adela?
Adela?
PONCIA. *(At the door.)* Open the door.
BERNARDA. Open the door! Don't think the walls will hide
your shame.
MAID. *(Entering.)* All the neighbors are up!
BERNARDA. *(In a low voice, but like a roar.)* Open the door, or
I'll break it down! *(Pause. Everything is silent. She walks away from
the door.)* Adela! *(La Poncia throws herself against the door. It opens
and she goes in. As she enters, she screams and backs out.)* What is it?
PONCIA. *(Puts her hands to her throat.)* May we never die like
that! *(The sisters fall back. The Maid crosses herself. Bernarda screams
and goes forward.)*
BERNARDA. Aaaarrrgghhh!
PONCIA. Don't go in!
BERNARDA. No ... Pepe — you run, alive, in the darkness
under the poplar trees, but, one day, you'll fall. Cut her down!
Carry her to her room and dress her in white. No one is to say
anything. Send word to toll the bells twice at dawn.
MARTIRIO. She's a thousand times happier to have what
she's had.
BERNARDA. And I want no tears. Death must be looked at
face to face. Tears are for when you are alone! We shall all of
us drown in a sea of mourning. The youngest daughter of
Bernarda Alba died a virgin. Did you hear me? Silence, silence
I said. Silence.

END OF ACT THREE

THE END

47

PROPERTY LIST

Bread and sausage (PONCIA)
Cane (BERNARDA)
Tray of little white jars (PONCIA)
Moneybag (PONCIA)
Fan with green and red flowers (ADELA)
Towels (ANGUSTIAS)
Handkerchief (BERNARDA)
Sewing materials (DAUGHTERS)
Embroidery materials (MAGDALENA)
Lace (MARTIRIO)
Plates and silverware (BERNARDA and DAUGHTERS)
Ring with pearls (ANGUSTIAS)
Glass of water (ADELA)
Lamb (MARIA JOSEFA)

SOUND EFFECTS

Bells tolling
Distant song (reapers' voices) with tambourine and
    carranacas
Distant shouts, a tumult
Shriek, clamor
Heavy blows against wall
Man's whistle
Gunshot
Thud

NEW PLAYS

★ **GUARDIANS by Peter Morris.** In this unflinching look at war, a disgraced American soldier discloses the truth about Abu Ghraib prison, and a clever English journalist reveals how he faked a similar story for the London tabloids. "Compelling, sympathetic and powerful." –*NY Times.* "Sends you into a state of moral turbulence." –*Sunday Times (UK).* "Nothing short of remarkable." –*Village Voice.* [1M, 1W] ISBN: 978-0-8222-2177-7

★ **BLUE DOOR by Tanya Barfield.** Three generations of men (all played by one actor), from slavery through Black Power, challenge Lewis, a tenured professor of mathematics, to embark on a journey combining past and present. "A teasing flare for words." –*Village Voice.* "Unfailingly thought-provoking." –*LA Times.* "The play moves with the speed and logic of a dream." –*Seattle Weekly.* [2M] ISBN: 978-0-8222-2209-5

★ **THE INTELLIGENT DESIGN OF JENNY CHOW by Rolin Jones.** This irreverent "techno-comedy" chronicles one brilliant woman's quest to determine her heritage and face her fears with the help of her astounding creation called Jenny Chow. "Boldly imagined." –*NY Times.* "Fantastical and funny." –*Variety.* "Harvests many laughs and finally a few tears." –*LA Times.* [3M, 3W] ISBN: 978-0-8222-2071-8

★ **SOUVENIR by Stephen Temperley.** Florence Foster Jenkins, a wealthy society eccentric, suffers under the delusion that she is a great coloratura soprano—when in fact the opposite is true. "Hilarious and deeply touching. Incredibly moving and breathtaking." –*NY Daily News.* "A sweet love letter of a play." –*NY Times.* "Wildly funny. Completely charming." –*Star-Ledger.* [1M, 1W] ISBN: 978-0-8222-2157-9

★ **ICE GLEN by Joan Ackermann.** In this touching period comedy, a beautiful poetess dwells in idyllic obscurity on a Berkshire estate with a band of unlikely cohorts. "A beautifully written story of nature and change." –*Talkin' Broadway.* "A lovely play which will leave you with a lot to think about." –*CurtainUp.* "Funny, moving and witty." –*Metroland (Boston).* [4M, 3W] ISBN: 978-0-8222-2175-3

★ **THE LAST DAYS OF JUDAS ISCARIOT by Stephen Adly Guirgis.** Set in a time-bending, darkly comic world between heaven and hell, this play reexamines the plight and fate of the New Testament's most infamous sinner. "An unforced eloquence that finds the poetry in lowdown street talk." –*NY Times.* "A real jaw-dropper." –*Variety.* "An extraordinary play." –*Guardian (UK).* [10M, 5W] ISBN: 978-0-8222-2082-4

DRAMATISTS PLAY SERVICE, INC.
440 Park Avenue South, New York, NY 10016 212-683-8960 Fax 212-213-1539
postmaster@dramatists.com   www.dramatists.com

NEW PLAYS

★ **THE GREAT AMERICAN TRAILER PARK MUSICAL music and lyrics by David Nehls, book by Betsy Kelso.** Pippi, a stripper on the run, has just moved into Armadillo Acres, wreaking havoc among the tenants of Florida's most exclusive trailer park. "Adultery, strippers, murderous ex-boyfriends, Costco and the Ice Capades. Undeniable fun." –*NY Post.* "Joyful and unashamedly vulgar." –*The New Yorker.* "Sparkles with treasure." –*New York Sun.* [2M, 5W] ISBN: 978-0-8222-2137-1

★ **MATCH by Stephen Belber.** When a young Seattle couple meet a prominent New York choreographer, they are led on a fraught journey that will change their lives forever. "Uproariously funny, deeply moving, enthralling theatre." –*NY Daily News.* "Prolific laughs and ear-to-ear smiles." –*NY Magazine.* [2M, 1W] ISBN: 978-0-8222-2020-6

★ **MR. MARMALADE by Noah Haidle.** Four-year-old Lucy's imaginary friend, Mr. Marmalade, doesn't have much time for her—not to mention he has a cocaine addiction and a penchant for pornography. "Alternately hilarious and heartbreaking." –*The New Yorker.* "A mature and accomplished play." –*LA Times.* "Scathingly observant comedy." –*Miami Herald.* [4M, 2W] ISBN: 978-0-8222-2142-5

★ **MOONLIGHT AND MAGNOLIAS by Ron Hutchinson.** Three men cloister themselves as they work tirelessly to reshape a screenplay that's just not working—*Gone with the Wind.* "Consumers of vintage Hollywood insider stories will eat up Hutchinson's diverting conjecture." –*Variety.* "A lot of fun." –*NY Post.* "A Hollywood dream-factory farce." –*Chicago Sun-Times.* [3M, 1W] ISBN: 978-0-8222-2084-8

★ **THE LEARNED LADIES OF PARK AVENUE by David Grimm, translated and freely adapted from Molière's Les Femmes Savantes.** Dicky wants to marry Betty, but her mother's plan is for Betty to wed a most pompous man. "A brave, brainy and barmy revision." –*Hartford Courant.* "A rare but welcome bird in contemporary theatre." –*New Haven Register.* "Roll over Cole Porter." –*Boston Globe.* [5M, 5W] ISBN: 978-0-8222-2135-7

★ **REGRETS ONLY by Paul Rudnick.** A sparkling comedy of Manhattan manners that explores the latest topics in marriage, friendships and squandered riches. "One of the funniest quip-meisters on the planet." –*NY Times.* "Precious moments of hilarity. Devastatingly accurate political and social satire." –*BackStage.* "Great fun." –*CurtainUp.* [3M, 3W] ISBN: 978-0-8222-2223-1

DRAMATISTS PLAY SERVICE, INC.
440 Park Avenue South, New York, NY 10016 212-683-8960 Fax 212-213-1539
postmaster@dramatists.com www.dramatists.com

NEW PLAYS

★ **AFTER ASHLEY by Gina Gionfriddo.** A teenager is unwillingly thrust into the national spotlight when a family tragedy becomes talk-show fodder. "A work that virtually any audience would find accessible." *—NY Times.* "Deft characterization and caustic humor." *—NY Sun.* "A smart satirical drama." *—Variety.* [4M, 2W] ISBN: 978-0-8222-2099-2

★ **THE RUBY SUNRISE by Rinne Groff.** Twenty-five years after Ruby struggles to realize her dream of inventing the first television, her daughter faces similar battles of faith as she works to get Ruby's story told on network TV. "Measured and intelligent, optimistic yet clear-eyed." *—NY Magazine.* "Maintains an exciting sense of ingenuity." *—Village Voice.* "Sinuous theatrical flair." *—Broadway.com.* [3M, 4W] ISBN: 978-0-8222-2140-1

★ **MY NAME IS RACHEL CORRIE taken from the writings of Rachel Corrie, edited by Alan Rickman and Katharine Viner.** This solo piece tells the story of Rachel Corrie who was killed in Gaza by an Israeli bulldozer set to demolish a Palestinian home. "Heartbreaking urgency. An invigoratingly detailed portrait of a passionate idealist." *—NY Times.* "Deeply authentically human." *—USA Today.* "A stunning dramatization." *—CurtainUp.* [1W] ISBN: 978-0-8222-2222-4

★ **ALMOST, MAINE by John Cariani.** This charming midwinter night's dream of a play turns romantic clichés on their ear as it chronicles the painfully hilarious amorous adventures (and misadventures) of residents of a remote northern town that doesn't quite exist. "A whimsical approach to the joys and perils of romance." *—NY Times.* "Sweet, poignant and witty." *—NY Daily News.* "Aims for the heart by way of the funny bone." *—Star-Ledger.* [2M, 2W] ISBN: 978-0-8222-2156-2

★ **Mitch Albom's TUESDAYS WITH MORRIE by Jeffrey Hatcher and Mitch Albom, based on the book by Mitch Albom.** The true story of Brandeis University professor Morrie Schwartz and his relationship with his student Mitch Albom. "A touching, life-affirming, deeply emotional drama." *—NY Daily News.* "You'll laugh. You'll cry." *—Variety.* "Moving and powerful." *—NY Post.* [2M] ISBN: 978-0-8222-2188-3

★ **DOG SEES GOD: CONFESSIONS OF A TEENAGE BLOCKHEAD by Bert V. Royal.** An abused pianist and a pyromaniac ex-girlfriend contribute to the teen-angst of America's most hapless kid. "A welcome antidote to the notion that the *Peanuts* gang provides merely American cuteness." *—NY Times.* "Hysterically funny." *—NY Post.* "The *Peanuts* kids have finally come out of their shells." *—Time Out.* [4M, 4W] ISBN: 978-0-8222-2152-4

DRAMATISTS PLAY SERVICE, INC.
440 Park Avenue South, New York, NY 10016 212-683-8960 Fax 212-213-1539
postmaster@dramatists.com   www.dramatists.com

NEW PLAYS

★ **RABBIT HOLE by David Lindsay-Abaire.** Winner of the 2007 Pulitzer Prize. Becca and Howie Corbett have everything a couple could want until a life-shattering accident turns their world upside down. "An intensely emotional examination of grief, laced with wit." *–Variety.* "A transcendent and deeply affecting new play." *–Entertainment Weekly.* "Painstakingly beautiful." *–BackStage.* [2M, 3W] ISBN: 978-0-8222-2154-8

★ **DOUBT, A Parable by John Patrick Shanley.** Winner of the 2005 Pulitzer Prize and Tony Award. Sister Aloysius, a Bronx school principal, takes matters into her own hands when she suspects the young Father Flynn of improper relations with one of the male students. "All the elements come invigoratingly together like clockwork." *–Variety.* "Passionate, exquisite, important, engrossing." *–NY Newsday.* [1M, 3W] ISBN: 978-0-8222-2219-4

★ **THE PILLOWMAN by Martin McDonagh.** In an unnamed totalitarian state, an author of horrific children's stories discovers that someone has been making his stories come true. "A blindingly bright black comedy." *–NY Times.* "McDonagh's least forgiving, bravest play." *–Variety.* "Thoroughly startling and genuinely intimidating." *–Chicago Tribune.* [4M, 5 bit parts (2M, 1W, 1 boy, 1 girl)] ISBN: 978-0-8222-2100-5

★ **GREY GARDENS book by Doug Wright, music by Scott Frankel, lyrics by Michael Korie.** The hilarious and heartbreaking story of Big Edie and Little Edie Bouvier Beale, the eccentric aunt and cousin of Jacqueline Kennedy Onassis, once bright names on the social register who became East Hampton's most notorious recluses. "An experience no passionate theatergoer should miss." *–NY Times.* "A unique and unmissable musical." *–Rolling Stone.* [4M, 3W, 2 girls] ISBN: 978-0-8222-2181-4

★ **THE LITTLE DOG LAUGHED by Douglas Carter Beane.** Mitchell Green could make it big as the hot new leading man in Hollywood if Diane, his agent, could just keep him in the closet. "Devastatingly funny." *–NY Times.* "An out-and-out delight." *–NY Daily News.* "Full of wit and wisdom." *–NY Post.* [2M, 2W] ISBN: 978-0-8222-2226-2

★ **SHINING CITY by Conor McPherson.** A guilt-ridden man reaches out to a therapist after seeing the ghost of his recently deceased wife. "Haunting, inspired and glorious." *–NY Times.* "Simply breathtaking and astonishing." *–Time Out.* "A thoughtful, artful, absorbing new drama." *–Star-Ledger.* [3M, 1W] ISBN: 978-0-8222-2187-6

DRAMATISTS PLAY SERVICE, INC.
440 Park Avenue South, New York, NY 10016 212-683-8960 Fax 212-213-1539
postmaster@dramatists.com www.dramatists.com